The Pitbull Guide

By Chad Zetrouer

Table of Contents:

Introduction

Despite all the myths and bad press the Pitbull gets, they are one of the best breeds available. When most people hear the word "Pitbull" they automatically think something along the lines of "That's a mean, aggressive dog." Unfortunately that's the stereotype Pitbulls seem to have. Pitbulls are by nature, very people friendly and will happily make friends with anyone they see.

Pitbulls are NOT guard dogs! They weren't bred to be guard dogs and if that's why you want one, I encourage you to get another breed. Pitbulls are bred to be people friendly. They have an extremely high drive and strong small game instincts.

I will talk more about Pitbulls and their history in the first chapter. But, first I want to let everyone know my reason for writing this book. Pitbulls are a highly misunderstood and mistreated breed. Most people want a Pitbull for the wrong reasons and because of this many Pitbulls end up abandoned or in the animal shelter. Hopefully this book will help people understand the breed better and show people that Pitbulls make for fantastic pets as long as the owner is willing to take on a little responsibility.

Pitbulls are different from other breeds and do require attention and proper care. Don't expect to get a low maintenance dog when you get a Pitbull because they're not. They require a lot of attention and proper training. They are high energy dogs that like to play and work. If you take the time to care for them properly, you will have one of the best friends/pets of your life.

In this book I will start off with the history of the breed and some basic information. It's good to know this information because it's what has made Pitbulls what they are today. Later in the book, I will teach the basics of training, followed by solutions to the most common behavioral problems Pitbull owners have. Keep in mind it's impossible for me go into every behavioral problem there is because there are far too many. However, I do provide several solutions to the most common problems. I will also teach you how create your own solutions by understanding why dogs have certain behaviors.

Chapter 1 – About Pitbulls/History

There are many names for the Pitbull. The most common are The Staffordshire Terrier, American Staffordshire Terrier, and American Pitbull. All of these dogs are the same or very similar. Some are just different varieties of the same breed. In fact, many people use these names interchangeably to describe any Pitbull.

Opinions on the exact history of the Pitbull vary but I will tell you the most accurate history that I know. Almost all agree that the Pitbull is a mix between a Bulldog and a Terrier. This is why they are sometimes referred to as Bull Terriers.

One common story goes back to Roman times when dogs were used in a sport called "Bull Baiting." As the Roman Empire spread, the best dogs of the sport were bred together and one distinctive dog began to emerge. This dog was called a Bulldog because it was used primarily for Bull Baiting. Bull Baiting was a brutal sport in which one or more Bulldogs would attack a bull. People thought this tenderized the bull's meat but that was just a lie to keep the sport going. There was also a similar sport called Bear Baiting in which bulldogs would attack a Bear.

At the peek of the Bull Baiting sport there were two primary breeds used, the Blue poll of Scotland and the Alunt from Ireland. Both were considered Bulldogs. By the 1800's after hundreds of years of selective breeding for the purpose of Bull Baiting, a new breed of dog emerged that slightly resembled the Pitbull. Soon after Bull Baiting was banned and made illegal because of its cruelty.

When Bull Baiting was made illegal people found a new brutal sport for dogs. This sport was called Ratting. In this sport dogs were placed into a pit filled with rats and then the dog that killed the most rats in given amount of time was the winner. This is where the first reference to the pit in Pitbull showed up. Not because of dog fighting. Terriers had a strong small game drive, and often excelled at this sport, but in an effort to breed better dogs the Terrier's which were primarily used for hunting small game, were bred with the Bulldogs. This resulted in a stronger more aggressive Ratting dog. It is believed that this cross breeding of Bulldogs and Terriers first began in Staffordshire England, hence the more politically correct name for Pitbulls, the Staffordshire Terrier. By mixing the Terrier with the Bulldog a new kind of Bulldog was created that was smaller and more agile.

When talking about Pitbulls a common term is "Gameness" or "Game", this is their strong will and instinctual refusal to quit. A game Pitbull will never back down from another dog or animal. This Gameness causes a

Pitbull to finish its task despite what happens to it, many will keep going until they die. Game also referred to their working ability because they would always be ready for work and never backed down from a job.

Shortly after Ratting began people noticed the strong game drive of this new breed and began to have dog fights. This started the relentless and precise breeding that resulted in today's Pitbull. The dogs were bred to be super gladiators that could destroy other dogs. Pitbulls ruled the fighting pit with little to no challenge from other breeds. Dog fighting was brutal and was eventually outlawed. Thankfully dog fighting isn't as popular as it once was but people do still use them for this cruel "sport."

Pitbulls were never bred to be guard dogs and are generally friendly with most humans unless mistreated and trained not to be. However, a Pitbull will often defend its master if it thinks the master is in danger. When they do defend their master you can expect a dog that's more tenacious and ferocious than any other breed on earth. Still they were not bred for this purpose and many will be very hesitant to ever attack a human. In fact, one of my friends was robbed at gun point a few years ago and his Pitbull ran and hid until the robber had left.

It is believed that the first Pitbulls arrived in America just before the Civil War although it's very possible that they arrived much earlier. In America they were used for various purposes including work, fighting, and companionship. By WWII the Pitbull had become America's dog mascot. They represented America's fierce determination and courage. Many were on posters during the war and they even helped soldiers in several wars. Later the Pitbull became the symbol for the RCA record company which featured a picture of a Pitbull looking at a record player.

Today Pitbulls have developed a bad name because of ignorant media coverage. Anytime there is a dog attack the dog is often referred to as a Pitbull even if it's a Golden Retriever. Because of the hype generated by the media, the Pitbull has been made illegal in some cities and there are even countries that wish to get rid of all the Pitbulls in their country!

There are still many people who realize what a fantastic breed this is and most Pitbull owners refuse to own another breed after owning a Pitbull.

Some notable Pitbull owners include Fred Astaire, Thomas Edison, Michael J. Fox, Madonna, Brad Pitt, Alicia Silverstone, Sinbad, President Roosevelt, Usher, Pink, Mary Tyler Moore, Tony Robbins, President Woodrow Wilson, Helen Keller, Serena Williams, and Jack Dempsy.

Here's what you can expect from the Modern Pitbull. The Pitbull is a medium sized breed that has a short smooth coat. Colors can vary greatly and are not considered important to breed identification. The Pitbull is very strong, intelligent, and hard working. They have a strong desire to please their owner and will go to extreme lengths to do so. Usually they have very muscular chests, legs, and jaws. Pitbulls also have wide jaws and well defined blockish heads.

Some people crop their Pitbulls tails and ears for looks but cropping the tail is not recommended because it affects their balance. Ear cropping is purely cosmetic and doesn't make a large difference. The nose of a Pitbull can be any natural color although most are black, red, blue or speckled.

A properly trained and socialized Pitbull will be extremely confident at all times. The Pitbulls natural agility allows them to climb trees almost as well as a cat. Pitbulls will go to great lengths to please their owner and are usually very good with children, however they should be watched at all times when around children because Pitbulls get so excited and playful that they may accidentally hurt a small child while trying to play.

Pitbulls can take a lot of pain and some are nearly impossible hurt. I've seen a Pitbull get hit by car and then get up and walk away like nothing happened. That was my friends Pitbull which is still healthy and happy years later even though a car going 20 to 30 mph hit it.

Pitbulls train well for any task because of their strong desire to please and their never give up attitude. Pitbulls can be trained for most dog jobs including hunting, drug sniffing, therapy, and many others. They train very easily and follow commands well.

Pitbulls are amazing pets, as long as they have the right owner. Anyone who wants to get a Pitbull should make sure they know about the breed before they get one because it takes responsibility to raise a Pitbull. With proper training and care you will be guaranteed a wonderful loving companion, but without proper training and care, a Pitbull can be a nightmare. A Pitbull can be very destructive if it doesn't get the proper amount of exercise and attention. This is very important if you plan on having a Pitbull. Pitbulls have seemingly endless amounts of energy and must be given a healthy, non destructive way to get rid of that energy or they will chew and dig to keep themselves entertained. They will also jump up on and play bite people if they aren't given enough exercise. I will tell you about several activities that Pitbulls love and excel at later in this book.

When a Pitbull is a puppy it needs to be socialized with

people and other animals to help insure that it doesn't become aggressive toward them later in life. It's helpful to take them on walks, in crowded areas so they can meet a lot of different people and other dogs. If your Pitbull is still young enough to not be a threat to other dogs, you may want to take it to a local dog park so that it can meet and play with a wide variety of other breeds.

Pitbulls require a lot of time and work to raise properly. So it's important that you have plenty of time to devote to socialization, training and exercise. Socialization is very important and plenty of time should be devoted to it. Pitbulls are naturally aggressive towards other dogs (especially of the same gender) and small animals. Whenever a Pitbull is around another animal it should be watched constantly no matter how well socialized it is. Socialization and training can help reduce their instinct to attack other animals but you should still be careful. I'm 6'1 and over 200 lbs but I remember it taking a lot of my strength to hold my friends 40 lb male Pitbull back from another male. Neither dog had ever been aggressive toward other dogs but when they saw each other it set something off in them. Pitbulls are incredibly strong and when they want something it's hard to hold them back. Training is useful here because if the Pitbull is trained well it will be more likely to listen to its owner.

If you want to get a Pitbull because it's a mean looking dog, you picked the wrong dog. There are plenty of other breeds that look meaner and are naturally more aggressive toward people than Pitbulls. Don't expect a Pitbull to be what it's not. It's also a bad idea to get a Pitbull as an outside only dog, because they need companionship and without people or something to do they will rip apart a yard at lightning speed. If you leave your Pitbull in your yard while you are gone, it MUST be secure because Pitbulls are magicians when it comes to escaping.

Chapter 2 – Pitbull Myths

There are many myths when it comes to Pitbulls. I will list them here for you so that you can help educate people ignorant people who try to trash them.

Pitbull Myths:

1. **Pitbulls are all mean and naturally aggressive towards humans.** This is absurd. Any dog can be trained to be mean. Pitbulls were bred to be friendly to humans but aggressive toward other animals. Most Pitbulls are extremely out going and friendly toward people, even strangers. This is why they are not good guard dogs.

2. **Pitbulls/Bulldogs have locking jaws.** A Pitbulls jaws work the same way as all other breeds. They have a very strong bite but their jaws do not lock. It's not possible.

3. **Pitbulls can hold on with their front teeth while chewing with their back teeth.** This is physically impossible and they cannot do this.

4. **Pitbulls are responsible for more attacks on humans than any other breed.** Outright lie (in my opinion). Most bites are from the "nicer" breeds, such as collies, retrievers, etc. The media just likes to cover Pitbull

attacks and will even call a German Shepard a Pitbull just because it sounds better. Some statistics do indicate that Pitbulls attack more than any other breed but me and many others believe this is due to misidentification and media hype.

5. **Pitbulls are only good for fighting.** Nope, they excel at many other things, such as working, companionship, playing, and most other things dogs do.

6. **Colors make a Pitbull more valuable or better.** With Pitbulls color doesn't matter very much. As far as shows go, color plays very little to no role in judging. Pitbulls can be just about any color. Most breeders charge extra for "Brindle", "Blue", or "Red Nose" Pitbulls. But there isn't any difference. It's really just a personal preference. There's a small amount of truth in the red-nose one because there is/was a line of fighting Red Nose's that were known for there gameness and fighting prowess. As these dogs were bred, they passed on there fighting ability as well as their red noses. So there is a very small amount of truth in saying that a red nose is more game or whatever else but since they've been bred with so many other dogs and aren't usually bred specifically for fighting anymore it doesn't make much, if any difference.

Those are just some of the most popular myths but there are plenty more, just remember to not believe everything you hear.

Chapter 3 – Similar Breeds

Many people own dogs they think are Pitbulls that aren't. People also associate their fighting prowess with size but that's incorrect because the smaller, more agile Pitbulls were favored in fighting. If you have a 100 pound "Pitbull" it's probably not a pure Pitbull. It is more likely one of the look-alikes or mixed with another breed.

The most common Pitbull imposters are the American Bulldog, Cane Corso, Presa Canerio, and Bandog. If you're looking for a guard dog that's intimidating as well as highly protective of his territory, I suggest the Cane Corso and Presa Canerio because both are formidable guard dogs. These dogs are huge and scary. They are good dogs but they have more of a protective instinct than most other dogs. I have one friend who bought a Cane Corso thinking it was a Pitbull. His Cane Corso is a wonderful dog that is very nice. The main thing his dog lacks is the gameness of a Pitbull.

Remember that Pitbulls are not supposed to be huge. They can be somewhat big depending on the breeding but not huge. Most Pitbull purists prefer the smaller Pitbulls that are more similar to the original dogs. In the last 50 years or so many people have bred Pitbulls with bigger dogs so they could say they had the biggest Pitbulls. By doing this they diluted the gameness of the dog but it's not to big of a deal unless you plan on entering your dog into shows. If it has Pitbull in it, it will retain many of the Pitbull traits. Remember Pitbulls are Mutts already and so are most other breeds. Usually mutts are healthier and live longer than pure breeds so don't immediately decide against a mix breed because they are great dogs also.

Here are some pictures of the look-alikes so you can tell the difference:

Bandog:

American Bulldog:

Cane Corso:

Presa Canerio:

Can you see how some people get these dogs mixed up with Pitbulls?

Chapter 4 – Picking the right Pitbull

If you decide that you want a Pitbull and think you have the necessary time and energy to care for one, you have two options. The first option is to buy a puppy and the second is to buy an adult. Both have their advantages.

If you are new to Pitbulls and worried about being able to train and care for one then your best option might be an adult from a Pitbull Rescue. These dogs are fully matured so you don't have to worry about socialization or temperament.

By the age of 3 they have pretty much completely matured and will retain the same personality for the rest of their lives. Pitbulls are a handful during adolescence because this is when they have the most energy. Few humans on earth have enough energy to keep up with a young Pitbull. That's why there are so many high energy activities for Pitbulls, so us slow humans can just get them started then sit back and watch. While this is a good choice, I still recommend a puppy because you can watch them grow up and who doesn't like puppies? It's important you consider getting an adult though because puppies will sometimes not show any aggression until they are older. With an adult you know right away if the dog is animal or human aggressive.

When picking a Pitbull adult or puppy there are some things you must look for:

Color is just a matter of preference and doesn't matter or affect the dog.

Eye color can vary also but the lighter more desired eye colors are considered less healthy.

Always look at the parents of a Pitbull puppy and ask to play with them. If the parents show aggression or a lack of confidence you should go elsewhere. Look at the parent's size and shape. Make sure they are Pitbulls and look healthy. Also ask if the parents have had any medical conditions such as hip dysplasia. If the parents look mistreated or questionable you should move on.

Sex is not greatly important when choosing a Pitbull. If you want to get two Pitbulls you should get one male and one female because Pitbulls of the same gender are more likely to fight. Males are slightly more territorial and dominant than females but neutering at an early age will almost completely eliminate any difference. So you should choose on preference only. Both male and female are very similar.

When buying a Pitbull puppy you should buy from a reputable breeder that cares enough to ask you about your home and makes sure that you are able to take care of a Pitbull. Backyard breeders often just breed for the money and don't care about temperament or aggression. Also consider trying to find a puppy or young Pitbull from a shelter or rescue because these are often good dogs that are in bad need of a loving home. Even an adult from a shelter or rescue is a good choice as long as it doesn't show any aggression. If a breeder doesn't care about whether or not you will provide a good home for the puppy then you should move on and find someone who does. Ethical breeders only breed the correct traits and make sure that all the puppies end up in good homes.

Other than that just pick the puppy or adult that you like the most or feel a connection to. As long as you are willing to put the time and work in, you will get an amazing dog.

Spaying and Neutering. Whether you decide to spay or neuter your Pitbull is up to you. Some people think that neutering a male will cause his muscles to not fully develop. If you are concerned about this I recommend you wait until your male is at least one year old before neutering him. Un-neutered males have a tendency to seek out females in heat and to roam; they also have more trouble concentrating on their task when a female is around. If you have a problem with your male Pitbull running away it's probably because he smells a female in heat and the best solution is to get him neutered.

Some people think that spaying a female can cause the female to become more aggressive because of the extra testosterone. If your female already shows aggression of any kind you may not want to spay her but otherwise it doesn't matter much.

Personally I recommend you neuter your male within the first year and talk to your vet and decide on whether or not to spay your female. But it's still purely a matter a preference. Each option has its pros and cons. I think it's more important and beneficial to neuter a male because there are a lot more pros than cons. The best thing to do is to talk the options over with your vet and then decide for yourself.

Chapter 5 – Proper Nutrition

It's important that your Pitbull gets the proper nutrition so that he can grow to his full potential and be healthy. Opinions vary on this subject but here are some good guidelines.

- Feed puppies 3 to 4 times a day and feed adults twice a day.

- If you have more than one dog, you should feed them separately because they may fight over the food.

- Don't rush a Pitbull puppy's growth by over feeding it. Let it grow at a normal pace and it will be healthier when it's fully grown.

- Never over feed a Pitbull. This can cause a condition called stomach torsion which is dangerous and possibly fatal.

- Feed at the same times every day so the dog knows when it's time to eat.

- Keep you Pitbulls food bowl clean and wash it regularly.

- Go easy on fatty treats so your dog doesn't become overweight.

- Ask your vet to recommend a dog food for your dog based on breed and age. Your vet knows better than anyone which foods are best.

- Make sure your Pitbull likes his food.

- Leave your Pitbull alone while eating and don't allow children to go near a Pitbull while eating because it could be unsafe if a child gets in the way of a Pitbull and its food.

- Dogs primarily use Fat for fuel, which means the Fat content of there food is a more important factor than the Protein. If your dog is extremely active then you should feed it foods with a high fat content and if your dog doesn't have many chances for exercise you should give them food with low fat content.

- If your Pitbull is too hyper, you are probably feeding it a food with to much fat or protein. To correct this you should switch to a dog food with about 12-14% fat and around 15% protein. Keep in mind Pitbulls are naturally energetic, so don't expect them to just lie around all day.

- When choosing a dog food for your Pitbull you should look at three things:

- The primary ingredient of the food, fat content, and protein content.

- First what is the primary ingredient in the food? Make sure it's not some kind of grain or vegetable. After all dogs are meat eaters not vegetarians!

- Look for food with a fat to protein ratio of around 15 fat to 20 protein. This means the food should have about 15 % fat and 20 % protein. If your dog is really active and works every day you will need to add some fat to the mix to supply your dog with more energy. To do this you can give them a tablespoon or two of vegetable oil or mix in some raw fatty hamburger. Yes it's ok for dogs to eat raw meat. Many people used to and some still do feed their dog only raw red meat. However, you should probably stay away from feeding them raw chicken and possibly even pork (although pork is much safer today than it used to be). Beef is really the best option.

- Don't buy expensive high performance foods unless your dog works most the day and needs all of that protein and energy. Also you can usually find foods with similar content as the expensive brands for much cheaper. Only feed your Pitbull foods with at least 12% or more fat. But again, not more than 20% if your dog isn't extremely active.

- If you give your dog table scraps make sure not to give them any cooked bones. Only give them raw bones because cooked bones can splinter and hurt your dog.

- Some Pitbulls can get picky about their food. I can't blame them. Would you want to eat that dry dog food? If you have problems with them not wanting to eat a certain kind of food you can mix in a little bit of milk, a raw egg, or even a tablespoon of mayo. This will make it more appealing to them.

Those are just some basic tips on feeding. Some dog foods are better than others but it's best for your vet to recommend which ones. Pitbulls with too much energy due to lack of exercise or food with too much fat or protein often have behavior problems such as jumping up on people, nipping, and destroying the house or yard.

Chapter 6 – Training

Training is very important if you have or are thinking of getting a Pitbull. Generally Pitbulls aren't a dominant breed. This means that you don't have to "show them who's boss", because they always strive to please their owner. Pitbulls are not like some other breeds that will challenge family members for dominance. Pitbulls are sensitive emotionally. I will tell you from personal experience that spanking or physical correction does not work with Pitbulls because they have such an incredible tolerance to pain. To really cause them any pain you would have to use force so extreme it would be horribly cruel.

This also rules out "training collars" or other pain correction devices. I also advise you to not put a heavy chain-like collar on your Pitbull. Some Pitbull owners think this builds strength and makes them look cool but it can damage their spine. Just use regular flat buckle collars.

-Good and Bad Training-

The oldest and most common training method is based on correction and punishment. Usually this type of training uses a lot of yelling, spanking, and jerking on a leash. All of these "corrections" involve punishment. This is partially effective because animals and humans try to avoid pain and discomfort.

One reason this method is badly flawed is because it often makes your dog fear you, which could eventually lead to more severe behavior problems like biting and aggression. Another problem with this method is that dogs usually don't know why they are being punished. If the correction doesn't come during or immediately after the unwanted behavior, the dog won't even know why it was punished.

A simple example of this method backfiring is people who can't get their dog to come to them when they call it. I see this all the time and can't help but laugh when I see someone running around outside trying to catch their dog because it won't come when called. This is another problem that is incredibly easy to fix.

You see when the owner finally catches their dog or the dog comes to them, the owner immediately punishes it for not coming earlier. However, from the dog's point of view, it is being punished for letting the owner catch it or actually going to the owner. So what the owner is actually doing is teaching the dog not to come when called and not to let the owner catch it, which makes the problem progressively worse. Put your self in the dog's place. Would you come if you got punished for it every time?

Here's the basis for all training:
When a behavior is rewarded, it will begin to happen more often. When a behavior is punished, it will happen less often.

Another important thing you should know is that the reward or punishment needs to happen during or immediately after the act for it to have any effect. In the previous example the owner thought he was punishing the dog for not coming when he was actually punishing it for coming.

If rewarded behavior happens more often and punished behavior happens less often, it's easy to think that the best training would involve equal amounts of both. However this isn't true. When training involves punishment, it makes the act of trying to learn undesirable for the dog. The dog will not want to train and learn new things if the process involves punishment. Instead the dog will try to avoid training and when forced to learn new things it will only learn enough to avoid the punishment.

When you use positive training methods that don't involve punishment, dogs learn much faster, remember their training longer, and become so enthusiastic about training that they will often try to get you to train them. They start to enjoy training and learning new things. On top of that you will also find that your relationship with your dog will become much better.

Before I go any further I should define some of the terms I will be using:

Positive Reinforcement – This is a reward that reinforces a behavior and makes that behavior happen more often. The reward can be a treat, praise, petting, etc.

Negative Reinforcement – Anything that causes discomfort or pain that ceases when the behavior ends. All negative reinforcers involve some kind of punishment.

While Negative Reinforcement and Punishment are somewhat similar, they are not the same thing. The difference between Negative Reinforcement and Punishment is that a Negative Reinforcement happens during a behavior and stops when the behavior stops, while punishment usually happens long after the behavior has stopped and thus has no effect on the behavior.

Let's look at the example of a boss yelling at an employee for writing a bad sales report. The boss is punishing the employee for the unsatisfactory work. His yelling cannot change the quality of that report, and probably won't have much effect on the next one. What it will do, is teach the employee to avoid his boss and at best, write the next sales report just good enough to avoid being yelled at. It will not make the employee want to perform better and may even cause the employee to resent his boss and his work.

A good example of a negative reinforcement is one of those Invisible Fence setups. These have a wire that you put around the area where you want your dog to stay and a collar to put on your dog. When your dog gets close to the wire, it will hear a warning sound and then if it continues toward the wire it will get a shock. After a few shocks the dog will learn that the warning sound always comes before the shock and will not keep walking when it hears the warning from then on. Your dog will learn that it can avoid the shock by stopping when it hears the warning (without the warning it would be cruel because the dog would have no way to avoid the shock). Because the shock comes during the unwanted behavior and because the dog can prevent it from happening by stopping when it hears the warning, this is a Negative Reinforcement.

While Invisible fences work well with many breeds they can be inconsistent when used for Pitbulls. Personally, I dislike all training collars that attempt to correct behavior problems with punishment.

Let's go back to the example of the boss yelling at his employee for writing a bad Sales Report. What if, instead of yelling at the employee, the boss started actively looking for good work done by the employee and when the boss saw the good work, he would reward it with praise, compliments, or perhaps a free lunch with the boss at a local restaurant? Try to put your self in the employee's shoes for a minute. Would this make you want to do better quality work? Would you have a better relationship with your boss? Would you put in a little extra effort on your Sales Reports in hopes of another reward? Of course!

Which business do you think would be more successful? The one with the boss that yells at employees for low quality work or the one with the boss that rewards employees for good work? That's Positive Reinforcement.

This leads us to the most effective and powerful training method available which is Positive Reinforcement Training. The common name for this type of training when applied to dogs is "Clicker Training." The reason it's called

Clicker Training is because of the "Clicker" used to mark behaviors. Clicker Training can be used to teach a dog to do just about anything.

The reason a clicker is used is because you usually can't get the treat to the dog at the *exact* moment of the behavior which makes using just treats less effective. In order for any training to be highly effective it must let the dog know exactly what is being rewarded. That's where the clicker comes in. The clicker is a little noise maker that you click during the behavior that will be rewarded.

The "Marker" doesn't have to be a clicker. It just needs to be something that can instantly let your dog know that what it's doing at that moment will get a reward. This could be a beep, flashing light, or whatever else. While you can use something else, it's probably better to just run up to the pet shop and pick up a few clickers, they're cheap and they are the accepted, popular way of doing it.

For a Clicker to work, your dog must associate the click with the later reward of say a treat. The reward can be anything as long as the dog sees it as a reward. If your dog just ate and is full, it might not see a treat as a reward. The reward could also be praise, petting, or possibly even a toy the dog enjoys. Treats work well but you should make sure the treat is small enough that the dog can eat it quickly and look to you for more. If the dog has to spend a minute eating the treat it will make the training more time consuming and less effective.

Before you can start clicker training your dog, you must first teach it that clicks are followed by treats. To do this, you should click, and then give your dog a treat several times so that he learns he will get a treat after he hears the click.

Another tip is that the clicker becomes more effective when paired with multiple rewards. So instead of just a click and treat, you should click, treat, praise, and pet. After you have associated the click with getting a treat, you should never click unless you are rewarding a behavior. If you don't follow the click with a treat, or if you overuse the clicker, it may become less effective.

A common myth about Clicker Training is that you must always click and treat for the learned behavior but that's completely wrong. Once your dog learns the trick or desired behavior, you can stop using the clicker and just give it a little praise instead.

Here's how you would teach your dog to "Sit" using clicker training. First you should get some treats, put them into your pocket and get the clicker out. Now it's best that you don't force your dog to sit or trick him into sitting. Instead, stay close and keep an eye on him. When you see him sitting you should click the instant his butt touches the ground and then give him a treat (you don't do it earlier because you may teach him to half sit). He won't know why he's being rewarded quite yet, so you need to keep watching and keep clicking and treating. This is the longest part of clicker training because it sometimes takes a dog anywhere from 10 minutes to 10 days to realize that what he's doing is earning him a click and treat. Once he does realize it, you will likely be able teach him tricks at a pace you've never dreamed of.

Now you will start seeing your dog sitting a lot more often in hopes of getting a reward. This is the time to start giving the command "Sit." With the treat and clicker handy, you should continue watching for your dog to sit and as soon as you see the behavior starting to begin (his butt starts going down toward the floor), you should say "Sit", click the instant his butt touches the ground, and give him a treat. Keep doing this, but try to get the "Sit" command in earlier and earlier until it comes before the act of sitting. Now you should be able to say "Sit" and your dog will sit.

The next step is to teach your dog that he will only get a reward when he sits after you give the command. To do this you should stop rewarding him when he sits without you giving the command and only click and treat when he sits after the command "Sit." Sometimes this will confuse the dog a little bit for a while but it's usually not long before he will understand the "Sit" means sit.

Now that you've got that down, other tricks such as Lay Down, Roll Over, Speak, and others will be very easy to teach using the same method. Some People have been able to teach their dog Sit, Down, Speak, and High Five in less than 24 hours after the dog learns its first trick with Clicker Training. This is because the dog learns that a click means you like the behavior currently being displayed. Basically the dog learns how to learn, and once you get past that, it gets very easy and very quick.

Chapter 7 – Behavioral Problems

All breeds of dogs are prone to behavioral problems. The most common problems are barking, biting, jumping up on people, and destructive behavior. There's usually a complex reason for each problem. The good news is that most problems can be solved pretty easily if you know how.

We already learned that excess energy and boredom often lead to behavioral problems but I think I should explain it some more. Pitbulls are high energy dogs and there's nothing we can do to change that fact, however we can keep their energy at a manageable level with proper diet and exercise. The main reason Pitbulls have too much energy is because their owners don't give them enough exercise. It's really not that hard to set aside thirty minutes to an hour a day to exercise your dog. I will give you some great things to do with your Pitbull in the next chapter, but there's no excuse for buying a Pitbull and then keeping it locked up in a house all day without giving it some way to release its energy.

Keeping a Pitbull outside all the time isn't a solution either, because Pitbulls need companionship and without a human presence they will get bored and probably dig and chew until your yard looks like the site of an epic battle. If you manage your Pitbulls food (Fat and Protein content) and you take time everyday to play with and exercise your Pitbull, you will have far fewer problems and you'll be happier.

-Fixing Behavior Problems-

When it comes to fixing behavior problems there are seven main methods for doing it. Some of these methods work great, while others can often cause more problems. I'll tell you about each one and give you an example of its use so you can better understand how to apply these methods to your situation.

Seven Methods for Fixing Behavior Problems:

- Punishment

- Negative Reinforcement
- Extinction
- Train an Incompatible Behavior
- Train a Command for the Behavior
- Shape the Absence of the Behavior
- Change the Motivation

Punishment

This is the most common method people use to modify behavior. Unfortunately it's also the least effective. We already covered Punishment in the last chapter so you should already have a good idea of what it is. The problem with punishment as a tool for modifying behavior is that it usually comes well after the behavior has happened and is over. Whether you're training Dogs or Humans, the correction must come during or immediately after the behavior for it to be effective.

When people punish their dog, it is often out of anger, or to get revenge for something the dog did. That's not only cruel but it's a waste of time. The major draw back to Punishment is that it often leads to resentment and fear, which can cause aggressive behavior later on. This method of fixing behavior problems should **not** be used.

Negative Reinforcement

A negative reinforcer is any type of uncomfortable or painful stimulation that can be avoided by a change of behavior. When you avoid the bathroom at the gas station because it smells bad, the smell is the negative reinforcer. By nature, all negative reinforcer's contain some kind of punishment that goes away when the unwanted behavior stops. The removal of the punishment can be seen as a positive reinforcement.

While negative reinforcement does have some good uses, it is not as effective as positive reinforcement. A human example of negative reinforcement is a parent nagging their child to clean their room. The nagging is the negative reinforcer which stops when the child cleans the room. Another result of this is that the nagging parent gets a positive reinforcement for nagging because it gets the desired result, which makes the parent more likely to nag in the future.

Here's a useful trick that uses negative reinforcement. If you have problems with your dog jumping up on the sofa or bed or maybe digging through the trash, try this… Get a spray bottle and fill it up about half way with water. Get some Lemon Concentrate or Vanilla Extract and put a little bit in the bottle and shake it up. Now spray your dog in the face with it for no reason. He should be a little shocked and should dislike the smell of it. All you have to do now is spray anything you don't want your dog to mess with. You can spray the trash can, around the bed and sofa, or whatever else. Your dog will associate the smell with the uncomfortable experience of being sprayed in the face and will avoid the areas where the smell is present. You might need to respray every couple months to keep the smell on those objects. It's not the "best" solution but it does the job without much punishment.

Negative Reinforcement should be avoided most the time. There are times when some mild negative reinforcement will help but you should try the more positive methods first.

Extinction

Extinction is when a behavior dies out naturally because the reward for the behavior has been removed. An example of this would be a dog that has the habit of begging for food while you eat. In this case you should let it beg but never give in and give it any food. The dog will eventually realize that the behavior of begging doesn't get rewarded and will stop begging. It's important to note that this will only work if you never give your dog any food because even a very rare reward will keep the behavior going.

A human example would be a child throwing a temper tantrum, the best way to end that behavior is to ignore it. At first it will get worse but eventually if you just ignore it, the child will soon learn that the behavior of having a tantrum is no longer rewarded and the behavior will end.

If your dog barks when the telephone rings, you can use Extinction to fix that problem also by removing the reward. First we need to find out what the reward for barking when the telephone rings is. The most obvious reason is because it frightens the dog and then the dog barks to make it stop or "go away." You answer the phone and the ringing sound goes away. What happens is your dog thinks that its barking made the phone stop ringing and is rewarded for the barking. The easy fix for this one is to desensitize your dog to the phone ringing and remove the reward of you answering it. Just use a cell phone or have someone else call you and then let the phone ring non-stop until your dog gives up and stops barking.

Once your dog stops barking, give it a treat to reinforce "not barking while the phone is ringing." To make this more effective I suggest you also ignore the phone and pretend like you don't hear it because you want to make the dog understand that the ringing is normal and nothing to fear.

Because nipping is usually an attention seeking behavior we can use Extinction to get rid of it. This is especially true in some puppies, because they nip trying to get your attention (Sometimes it can also be teething). The first thing you should try is to remove the reward of attention and ignore the nipping. To do this you should simply stand up and walk away when your puppy starts nipping you. Your puppy should soon stop this behavior because it no longer gets the desired reward.

For extinction to work it must be used on a reward seeking behavior in which you can remove the reward. Extinction will not work on self rewarding behaviors.

Train an Incompatible Behavior

This is when you train a behavior that is physically incompatible with the unwanted behavior. Your dog can't do the unwanted behavior if it is trained to do something else at the same time. An example of this is a dog that barks and growls at the door when someone knocks or rings the door bell. What you would do is train the dog to do something else when it hears someone at the door. The incompatible behavior you train could be lying down, sitting, going to another room, or anything else. You would first train the behavior and then make the doorbell or knocking sound the command.

This same thing could be used with all kinds of different problems. A few that come to mind are begging and jumping up on people.

Put the Behavior on Command

This one's pretty cool and effective. The idea behind it is to train your dog to do the unwanted behavior on command and then train it to **only** exhibit that behavior on command.

Let's look at the example of a dog that barks a lot. First

you need to figure out when it barks the most and get your treats and clicker ready at that time. Start by rewarding the barking with a click and treat. After doing that a few times, start working in the command "Speak" as close to the beginning of the barking as you can and keep on clicking and treating.

Continue doing this until you can say "Speak" before your dog barks. Once you can give the command and get a bark reliably, stop rewarding any barks that don't come after a command and throw in the command "Speak" every once in a while to let your dog know that it still gets rewarded for barking after the command.

Now you should have your dog trained to bark on command and not any other time. The reason this works is because the dog starts expecting a reward for barking, and learns that it only gets the reward when it barks after the "Speak" command. After that there's no reason to bark if it knows there will be no reward.

This one doesn't work 100% of the time on some behaviors because the original reward for the behavior is to strong. For example, this may or may not work on a dog that barks at squirrels or passing cars because it is already getting a reward when they leave after the barking. The dog thinks that it's barking scared them off and is thus rewarded. This is still a very useful method and it can deliver great results.

Shape the Absence of the Behavior

Here's a good all around method for improving your dog's behavior. What you do is reward any behavior that isn't the unwanted behavior and then when you see the unwanted behavior, don't give a reward. Your dog will figure something is going on and should pick it up that the other behaviors are rewarded but the unwanted behavior isn't. The idea is that you rewarding your dog for not showing the unwanted behavior. When you notice the absence of bad behavior, reward that absence.

In the case of the begging dog, you could watch it until it loses interest or does anything else besides beg and then reward that behavior. So if the dog stops begging and walks away or goes to eat some of its own food, immediately click and give it a treat.

Here's an example of using this method combined with Extinction. If your dog is jumping up on people, you can use these two methods to quickly solve the problem. Next time your dog jumps up on you, turn your back to him and ignore him. While you're doing this, keep an eye on him without directly looking at him. The second you see him put all four feet back on the ground, turn around and reward him with a treat and a lot of praise.

This works because when you ignore the behavior of jumping up, you are removing the reward of attention and petting and when you reward the behavior of having all four feet on the ground, you are rewarding the absence of the jumping up behavior.

Change the Motivation

Many, if not most dog behaviors are self rewarding. For this to work, you first need to find out what the motivation for the behavior is.

Why is your dog barking?
Dog's often bark because they're lonely and bored. To change the motivation, you could give it a lot of exercise during the day so that it is tired and sleeps more at night.

Why does your dog jump up on you when you get home?

To get attention, and to be petted. Remove the excitement by ignoring your dog for 10 minutes before you leave and for 10 minutes after you get home each day. This way you don't scare the dog when you leave by acting sad and saying things like "I'll be back, don't worry."

Why does your dog beg?

Because it is hungry. Change the motivation by feeding your dog before or while you eat.

Each of these methods has its good points and bad points. Some methods are better than others, depending on the problem. It's up to you to be creative and figure out which will work best for your situation. If one doesn't work you can try another. You will probably find that many problems require a combination of these methods.

Separation Anxiety Disorder

There's another common cause for behavior problems that doesn't really fit any of those methods well. That cause is Separation Anxiety Disorder which is a condition where dogs get scared and anxious when separated from their owner.

Everything from barking to destructive behavior can be attributed to Separation Anxiety. One common cause of Separation Anxiety is owners that make their absence a big deal by saying sad goodbyes and then overly happy hellos when they get home. Dogs can't understand what their owners say but they can usually pick up on the emotions of their owner. So when you act sad before leaving, there's a good chance you are scaring your dog and making it think there is something to worry about.

Like I pointed out earlier, you should try to ignore your dog for ten minutes before your leave and for ten minutes after you get back home. This way you don't make your dog think that there is something to worry about.

Another promising new solution to this problem is D.A.P. or Dog Appeasing Pheromone. Before I can explain what D.A.P. is, I must first explain what pheromones are. Pheromones are a form of chemical communication between animals. Most, if not all animals have some use for pheromones even insects and humans have and use pheromones.

Pheromones act much like a smell except that pheromones often affect behavior (very strongly in some instances). D.A.P. is released by female dogs that have recently given birth and it continues to be released until the puppies are done nursing. The reason for this is because D.A.P. makes the puppies feel safe and calm when around their mother. It also helps to form a stronger connection between the mother and her puppies.

What makes D.A.P. appealing is that research shows it works on adult dogs as well as puppies. While I'm still unsure if it's effective for 100% of dogs, many if not most people find that it does have a positive effect on their dog's behavior.

So if your dog exhibits destructive behavior only when you are not home. There is a good chance it may have Separation Anxiety Disorder. Some of the things dogs with this disorder will do include, chewing things they are not supposed to, barking, and peeing in the house. If you suspect your dog has this condition you should first try the technique I described above where you ignore your dog for ten minutes before you leave and after you get home. If that doesn't solve the problem, you may want to buy some D.A.P. from the local

Pet Store or Vet's Office and give it a try.

-Dog Problems Solved-

While I can't cover every possible problem, I will make an effort to provide solutions for the most common ones. Based on the email I receive, these appear to be the ones that people have the most trouble with.

If your specific problem isn't covered here, you can use the information from the previous chapter to create your own solution. All of the solutions I provide are based on the seven methods that I wrote about in the last chapter.

Not Coming When Called

One of the most common and fundamental problems people have with their dog is not being able to get it to come to them when called.

Coming when called is probably the most important thing you will teach your dog. It might even save their lives at some point. A properly trained dog should come to you every time you call it, no exceptions.

Here's a very common situation:

A dog and it's owner are outside and the owner calls for it to come, but it doesn't come, instead it starts a game of "catch me if you can." This is followed by the owner running around calling and chasing the dog getting more and more upset with each step.

When the owner finally catches the dog they

immediately proceed to spank and yell at it... "NO" whap "NO"

Now imagine what the dog is thinking at this point. It finally went to it's owner or allowed it's self to be caught and now it's getting punished.

From the dog's point of view it's being punished for coming. The most basic rule of training is that "rewarded behaviors will happen more often and punished behaviors less often."

So every time you repeat the above scenario with your dog you are training it to not come to you. The complete opposite of what you wanted.

Getting your dog to come when called is one of the easiest things teach a dog. You simply need to reward the behavior of coming.

Here's how you do it:

You will be teaching your dog the "Come" command. You will say "Fido, Come" and your dog will come to you (replace Fido with your dogs name).

The key here will be the reward. Every time your dog comes to you say "Good Dog" in an excited enthusiastic voice while at the same time giving your dog a small treat or piece of dog food that your dog likes.

But before you can reward your dog for coming, you need to get it to come. There are many ways to do this, but the most effective is to use your dogs hunger to your advantage.

Pick a day to do this training and do not give your dog

any treats before training. Then wait until the normal time your dog eats and pick that time to go outside and start training.

Fill your pockets with small but good treats or just little pieces of dog food. It's important that they are small so they don't fill your dog up before you finish training.

Once outside let your dog move a short distance away from you, then pull out a treat, hold it out so your dog can see it, and say "Fido, Come" in a happy, excited voice. Do this all as one movement so your dog connects the command with the treat being offered.

Your dog should come to you and when it does you reward it with the treat and praise.

Now let your dog move off again and repeat. Continue to repeat this about 20 times before ending the training session. As your dog improves, you can start letting it move further away, or using the command while it is busy doing something else.

That will work for 90% of the dogs out there but for particularly stubborn dogs there is another way to do it...

What you will need to do is carry treats with you all the time and take advantage of the times when your dog naturally comes to you. Whenever your dog does come. Immediately say "Fido, Come" and reward the behavior with a treat and praise.

Eventually your dog will make the connection that it is getting the treat when you say "Come" and it comes to you.

A day or two of this and you can move outside for the training exercises above.

To further reinforce the behavior, you can turn it into a game:

Have two people with treats go outside and stand about 20 to 30 feet apart. Now take turns calling and rewarding the dog. Do it so the dog is running from person to person, only stopping at each person for a few seconds.

This game will further reinforce your training by making it fun for your dog (increasing the reward).

Digging

Why do dogs dig?

- It feels good.
- It creates a cool resting place.
- They smell things under the ground.
- It relieves stress.
- They're lonely.
- They don't get enough exercise.
- They're trying to escape under the fence.

As you know the solution to a problem often depends on the cause. You should be able to figure out the cause pretty quickly just by looking at the list above. For example if the holes are near your fence, your dog is probably trying to escape. If the holes are randomly spaced around the yard and your dog only digs when you're not around, it's probably caused by boredom, loneliness, or stress.

Before I cover any of the solutions I should first tell you what not to do:

- Do not fill the holes with water and push your dogs head into them.
- Do not punish your dog when you get home and find new holes.

If you think the digging is caused by loneliness or boredom, which are the most common causes, there are several things you can do to help stop the digging.

First you should try to minimize the time that your dog is left alone outside. You should also try to play with your dog more often and make sure it gets plenty of exercise. You should also get good toy like a Kong and smear some peanut butter inside it so that it will entertain your dog for a long time.

If you dog is attempting to escape by digging under the fence and it hasn't been spayed or neutered, then there is a good chance it smells another dog. This is especially common with male dogs, because they will do anything to get out if they smell a female in heat (which dogs can often smell from miles away).

There are a couple solutions for the escape artist dog, first you should consider getting your dog fixed but never rely on that as a 100% solution because it doesn't always work.

Another idea is to bury chicken wire along edges of your yard a foot or two below the fence. When your dog hits the chicken wire it won't feel good and it should prevent any further digging.

If your dog keeps digging in the same spot over and over, first try gathering some poop from the yard and burying it in the hole. That usually stops them from digging in that spot. If you still have trouble, try filling the hole with gravel and then covering it with a thin layer of dirt. The gravel makes digging less pleasurable and will discourage digging.

One solution I like for dogs that just enjoy digging or want a cool place to rest, is a sand box. This is almost the same thing as a kid's sandbox except you should make it as deep as possible (1 to 3 feet deep should be good). The idea is to train your dog to only dig in the sandbox. You can do this by taking them to it, getting them to dig, and then rewarding them. Dogs prefer the feeling of sand over most backyard soils so it shouldn't be too hard.

The idea is to reward your dog for digging in the sandbox, but ignore them when they dig elsewhere. It shouldn't take long for your dog to figure out that digging in the sandbox is a more rewarding behavior.

You should avoid leaving hoses or anything else your dog can chew and swallow in your yard because hose pieces can cause serious problems if your dog swallows them.

Another thing to avoid is any chemical yard treatment that may be harmful to your dog. That includes some fertilizers and especially insecticides.

Chewing

Chewing is a tough problem to solve because, like many other behavior problems, it's just something dogs love to do.

Dogs chew for several reasons:

- It feels good
- They're bored

- It relieves stress
- To seek attention

Most chewing cases can solved by providing a good alternative such as a chew toy and rewarding your dog for chewing on its toys as opposed to other things. Just reward your dog when you see him chewing on a toy. Then when your dog gets something you don't want him to chew on, like one of your shoes, take away the shoe and give him a toy. Then reward him when he starts chewing on the toy.

This is another problem that a Kong type toy can help because Kongs allow you to put food like peanut butter inside them so that they retain your dog's attention for longer. There's even a new gadget that releases Kongs at specified times throughout the day while your gone.

It's also a good idea to leave a toy in every room your dog might be in while you're gone so that it doesn't have to go far when looking for a toy.

Like I said before Chewing as well as a lot of other problems could be do to Separation Anxiety Disorder, which I covered earlier.

If your dog seems to prefer chewing on certain objects, you can try an Anti-Chew spray that's available at most pet stores. If you want to make your own anti-chew spray, just get a spray bottle and fill it with water, then add about a tablespoon of concentrated lemon juice or vanilla extract. Now take the spray and spray your dog in the face with it. That will shock your dog and your dog will associate that smell with the unpleasant experience of being sprayed. Now just spray the objects you want your dog to stay away from. While this usually works you should be careful not to spray it on to many things because the smell could end up punishing your dog all the time.

As with most problems, chewing can usually be lessened by giving your dog enough attention and exercise every day.

Barking

This is one of the most common complaints I hear. I think the reason for that is because barking can be more annoying than a lot of other problems, and most people think it is difficult to fix. Like chewing and digging, barking is another natural behavior for dogs. It's just as natural as a human speaking.

First, don't try any of the available Bark Collars because they usually don't work and can be cruel. The only exception, which I still don't like, is a citronella bark collar.

One of my favorite solutions for an excessive barker is to put the barking behavior on command like I talked about earlier. To do this you first need to teach your dog to bark on command. I know that sounds like a dumb thing to do but the idea is to teach your dog that when it barks on command, it gets a reward, and when it barks any other time it doesn't get a reward. Your dog will soon learn that barking without the command isn't rewarding and hopefully stop. Because I gave instructions on how to do this earlier I won't repeat it here.

Another common reason for barking is territorial. This happens when the dog sees someone walking by and barks at them because they are near or in the dog's territory. This ends up being reinforced when the person keeps walking. The best solution to this is to make it so your dog can't see anyone walking by. Putting the barking on command usually helps with this also.

If your dog barks when it's scared, such as when there's a thunderstorm. You can usually help this by exposing your dog to the things that scare it and rewarding it for staying calm so that it learns not to be afraid. I will cover this more in the next section.

Fears and Phobias

Many dogs have fears or phobias and they can cause all kinds of behavior problems. The most common is destructive behavior in the form of chewing or digging. Dogs do these things to comfort them selves when afraid.

Usually these fears can be avoided by good socialization when your dog is a puppy. Socialization is just exposing your dog to as many new things as possible and letting it know that it doesn't need to be afraid of them. It's especially important to expose puppies to as many people and other dogs as possible at a young age because it will affect their behavior for the rest of their lives.

The most common fears are riding in cars and thunder or loud noises. If your dog has a fear of riding in cars, you can solve that by slowing exposing your dog to the car and rewarding it for staying calm.

First you need to get your dog to the car. Do this by putting your dog on a leash and walking it up to about ten feet away from the car. If your dog doesn't show any fear, give it a treat and walk away from the car. A minute or two later walk your dog to about five feet away from the car. If it stays calm, give it a treat, praise it, and then walk away from the car again.

Depending on how bad your dog's fear of cars is, you may need to do this in shorter increments. Now you need to keep going the same way, little by little. Get your dog to stand outside the open car door. Then get it to get in to the car while remaining calm. Next close the door and reward your dog for remaining calm. Then start the car, reward your dog, and drive a short distance. While driving reward your dog every few minutes if it stays calm. The idea is to not only desensitize the dog to riding in the car but also to shape the absence of the fear.

For a little while after doing this you will need to reward your dog every time it gets into the car as well as at the end of the ride as a reward for staying calm. After a few weeks you should be able to stop with the food rewards and just use praise and petting.

Thunder and loud noises can be a little more difficult to deal with. This is a problem that can get progressively worse if left untreated. One problem that's somewhat common is that the dog will begin to fear people and objects that it associates the loud noise with.

If your dog sees a kid outside making loud noises it could start to associate kids with the fear and discomfort it experiences when it hears loud noises. This may lead to the dog fearing every kid it sees and possibly even fear biting.

There are only a few ways to help solve this problem. The most common way is by desensitizing the dog to the loud noises it fears. If your dog fears thunderstorms, you can get a tape of a thunderstorm and start by playing it at a low volume. If your dog doesn't get scared by the sound, reward it with a treat and praise. Now continue by slowly turning up the volume and rewarding your dog for staying calm along the way. Do that until the volume is about the same or louder than a real thunderstorm.

Unfortunately desensitizing doesn't always work. If you try it and don't see any results you should try to create a place for your dog to go when it gets scared. This place should be protected from the noises as much as possible. A common way to do this is to put an open crate in an interior bathroom and cover the crate with some towels so that it's dark. Just try to make it as comfortable as possible and it should provide some relief for your dog.

Poop Eating

Eating feces, which is also known as Coprophagia is a common behavior problem that dogs have. Other than being disgusting to people, eating poop usually doesn't cause any health problems, however you should try to keep your dog from eating other dogs poop or old poop because they can make your dog sick. While there hasn't been very much research into why dogs eat their own or even other dogs poop, there are some things that you can do to solve the problem.

There are quite a few theories on why dogs eat their poop. Some believe it is an attention seeking behavior because when the dog's owner sees it eating poop, they will usually yell at the dog. Many dogs see any attention, good or bad, as rewarding so that makes sense in some cases.

Others believe that it's a learned behavior. Dogs see other dogs or even their owners picking up (or eating) poop and learn to do it themselves. Then there are the more logical theories that dogs find it rewarding (maybe it tastes good?) or they just do it because they are hungry.

It has been found that dogs that are only fed once a

day, are more likely to eat their poop in an attempt to have more than one meal a day. This is because dogs prefer to have several meals a day as opposed to just one.

The most common solution to this problem is to make the poop taste bad. One product people use is called Forbid™ which is a powder you put on your dogs food, another is called Deter™ which is a pill you give your dog. Both make your dogs poop taste bad and hopefully stop the behavior.

Another common solution is to get your dog to associate something unpleasant with eating its poop. This is almost the same as using the products above. What you do is, put hot sauce (not to hot) on the poop in your yard or wherever your dog eats it and then let your dog eat it. Dogs usually hate hot sauce and after a few attempts at eating their Cajun Poop, they usually make the association and stop the behavior.

Overall, there are a few other things you should do to avoid the behavior. You should try to feed your dog at least twice a day because that has helped in some cases. You should also try to pick up or bury the poop often so there are fewer opportunities for your dog to eat it. If you believe your dog is doing the behavior to get attention, your best bet is to just ignore it and eventually the behavior will end because it is no longer rewarded (extinction).

Chapter 8 – Pitbull Exercise and Fun

Pitbulls love to exercise and play. Some of the things they can do are shocking. Because they have so much energy you must give them a way to use it in a non-destructive manner.

Here are some things Pitbulls enjoy:

Walking/Running - You should take your Pitbull on a long walk every day if possible. Make sure you have a good strong leash and use a muzzle if your Pitbull shows aggression toward other animals.

Tug of war – This is a fun way for you to interact with your Pitbull. Some say it's not good but I've always done it and had no problems. Just get a thick rope or toy and play.

Weight Pulling – Pitbulls excel at pulling. You can train them to do this pretty easily. All that's required to get started is a chest harness and something for them to pull. Usually an old tire works good to get them started. Just put on their pulling harness and then have them pull the tire around the yard for exercise. There are contests for this which have more rules but this is just for exercise purposes. Later you can buy more equipment so you can add more and more weight for them to pull. There are even little carts you sit in and then have them pull you like a sled dog. Just don't over work them. Make sure they get enough exercise but be sure to let them rest because they will often keep going as long as you tell them to and possibly hurt themselves.

Spring Pole/Rope – This is my favorite as well as most Pitbulls favorite activity. It's truly amazing to watch and will impress anyone that sees it. Later if you choose, there are competitions for this activity. I've never seen a Pitbull that doesn't love his rope. It's hard to get them to not go after it every time they see it.

Why do they do this? It's a direct link to their Bull Baiting days when the best hold a dog could get on a bull was on the nose. They would jump up and bite the bulls nose, which is one of the most sensitive areas of the bulls body then just hang there and not let go. This usually made the furious bull calm down and surrender. There is also a story that way back when, butchers used bulldogs to bring bulls to slaughter. You can imagine that it would be hard to move a bull and take it to its slaughter, so butchers had a bulldog that would jump up and bite the bull's nose and hang there. This then allowed the butcher to grab the dog and then guide the bull to its slaughter by pulling the dog as if it was a leash on the bull.

Later nose rings for bulls were developed for this purpose. I'm not sure if this story is 100% accurate but it makes sense. Now almost every type of Bulldog will exhibit the same type of behavior because it has been bred into them.

Constructing a springpole or rope swing is pretty easy. Most people simply hang a rope from a sturdy tree branch and then supply a hardy knot or other wide surface for the Pitbull to bite. If you don't have a tree branch suitable for hanging the rope you can build a simple rope swing from some 2x4's, 4x4's, concrete, and nails. Anywhere you can hang a rope that's sturdy enough to hold the dog's weight is fine.

It takes very little effort to teach a Pitbull how to use a springpole and they often immediately figure it out. If your Pitbull doesn't immediately go after it, then there are some things you can do to help teach them. After they do it once they will instinctually become pros at it. If you have a puppy, you can start by going from tug of war to actually picking them up off the ground a few inches and holding them there for long periods of time. This will help them develop the jaw strength necessary.

First start with your rope hanging down so that it's just above your Pitbulls head, then shake the rope right in front of your dog and tell him/her to get it. If that doesn't work try lightly tapping the rope against the side of his/her mouth. It shouldn't be very hard to get them to bite it and start playing tug of war with it. Next raise the rope so that it's at a height that would require your Pitbull to stand on its hind legs to get it. Shake the rope and tell your Pitbull to get it in an enthusiastic voice. After you have this, you should raise the rope again so that it's high enough for your Pitbull to hang without touching the ground. That's it. Soon you will be able to say "Get the rope!" and your Pitbull will immediately and happily go after it and then hang there and fight it for very long periods of time. I've seen one Pitbull hang for over 30 minutes before, and then after falling go right back up for more.

Some people will see this and think it's cruel but I assure you it's not. If anything it's cruel to have a Pitbull and not have a springpole. This is in there blood and they love it. My friend had a problem with his neighbors calling the police on him every time he took his Pitbull out to get on the rope. The neighbors were ignorant about Pitbulls and thought he was hanging the dog from a tree. The cops seemed to enjoy coming out and watching my friends dog get the rope. They would come almost weekly and say "are you hanging your dog again?" then laugh and spend a few minutes watching and talking before leaving.

As your Pitbull gets stronger and better at it you can raise the height of the rope so that your Pitbull has to jump higher. The highest I've seen a Pitbull jump (the height of the part it bites) is about 9 feet. That's pretty incredible to see. Don't raise it so high that it takes your Pitbull forever to get because that will make it too hard and no fun. Every once in a while you may want to test his jumping ability though.

Another important tip is to make sure you use rope and not a chain because a chain can hurt your Pitbull.

Treadmill – Another thing Pitbulls take to pretty easily is a treadmill. At first it may take them a little while to figure it out but after a while they will get it. There are even special tread mills made specifically for dogs. However, I suggest walking or running with your Pitbull, it's good exercise for both of you.

Soccer – Give your Pitbull a ball that can take some punishment and many Pitbulls will kick and chase it like there going crazy. It's a lot of fun to watch and Pitbulls love it. There are special balls available at pet stores that are more durable than flimsy soccer balls.

Pitbulls are excellent competitors in spring pole and pulling competitions. With some practice your Pitbull may be able to win some of these. Another great benefit to these exercises is that they rapidly build up your Pitbulls muscles.

There are many more fun activities. You will probably notice that your Pitbulls has a lot of little crazy things he or she likes to do. Just give them an outlet for their energy that's fun for both of you and you will have many years of fun with your Pitbull.

Chapter 9 – Laws and the Future

Because of the unjust, bad reputation Pitbulls have gotten from ignorant people and the media, they are now at risk of being banned in various areas all around the world. Cities, Counties, States, and even some Countries are considering something called Breed Specific Legislation against Pitbulls. Some Pitbull lovers are fanatical over this but all see it as a threat. It's the equivalent of racism since these new laws that people are trying to get passed focus on just one or a few breeds of dogs. They say that Pitbulls are dangerous but Dobermans are much more dangerous and so are German Shepard's and Chows.

One factor behind this legislation is that many criminals have Pitbulls and those Pitbulls are usually mistreated and never socialized so they tend to be more aggressive toward people. Another big reason is that very few people can actually identify a Pitbull. I bet 99% of Americans couldn't pick a Pitbull out of a line up, yet when they see a dog attack for just a few seconds they immediately know it's a Pitbull. The fact is that it's probably a Cane Corso, Presa Canerio, Mastiff, or some other similar breed and not a Pitbull. There's even one story where a news reporter reported a Pitbull attack then later when it was investigated, it was found to be a Golden Retriever! If you can't tell a Golden Retriever from a Pitbull you shouldn't be covering a story about a dog attack.

Some people call their dogs Staffordshire Terriers to help to keep people from labeling them as a Pitbull. It's really disgraceful how the breed that was once America's animal mascot has become an enemy.

It is true that Pitbulls are naturally aggressive toward other animals. That's in there genes, but they ARE NOT naturally aggressive toward humans. In fact they were bred to be naturally friendly toward humans.

Some insurance companies will not give you home insurance if you own a Pitbull. I'm not going to tell you to lie or do anything else illegal but many people get around this problem by saying their dog is a mutt, lab mix, or possibly even a Staffordshire Terrier.

If you are thinking of getting a Pitbull then you should be aware of your responsibility as an ambassador of the breed. I've changed many people's views about Pitbulls by simply introducing them to one. As soon as they see this dog that without hesitation runs up to them, tail wagging, and licking, they can't help but change their mind. They see that the only thing it wants is to play and be loved. It's actually funny to watch. A lot of people see a Pitbull and are automatically a little stand offish and scared of it, but the Pitbull just walks right over and tries to get them to play with it.

One solution is to shut down unethical breeders that churn out as many Pitbull puppies as they can and then sell them to anyone who has the money to buy one. These breeders could care less if the dog goes to an abusive or neglecting household. They don't care if it's dropped off at the pound as soon as it grows up and isn't a puppy anymore.

This also reminds me to tell you to try not to breed your Pitbull unless you already have several people that you know will give the puppies a good home. Then once you know you have several people that want one and can provide a good home, you can breed them.

Hopefully as more and more people see that this is a wonderful and loving breed they will change and begin to think differently about them.

Chapter 10 – Work for Pitbulls

Pitbulls are a very skilled breed and can handle about any task that other breeds can and can often do the task much better. Their strong desire to please and their never quit attitude make them perfect working dogs.

Here are just a few of the things Pitbulls are suited for:

- Pitbulls have proven to be great herding dogs when

properly trained.

- Pitbulls excel at Search and Rescue.

- Many people prefer Pitbulls for wild pig hunting. They are great at pinning a pig.

- Drug sniffing and police work is good for a Pitbull.

- Tracking, just like most other dogs, Pitbulls have a great sense of smell and can track well.

- Assisting disabled people. Pitbulls are excellent for this job!

- And just about anything else. Because they are so easy to train and are so eager to please they excel at almost everything. If another dog can do it good, a Pitbull can probably do it better.

While these stories don't have much to do with working Pitbulls, I wanted to share them here so that you could read them. Both of these stories are true or are believed to be true. Fictional names were used in the first story to preserve the privacy of those involved.

My Dog – My Savior

This story comes from a lady named Sarah in Louisiana. This story shows that even though Pitbulls aren't bred to be guard dogs, they can be when needed.

Every night Sarah took her Pitbull Jesus out for a walk. Tonight was no different, so she grabbed the leash and Jesus ran over so she could put the leash on him. As they were leaving the house Sarah noticed a strange man standing right outside her bedroom window. The man saw her as well yet he did not move. Startled and a little scared she told the man to leave. The man then moved toward her and attempted to grab the leash, but as soon as he did, Jesus leapt toward him and made the man step back. Then Sarah told the man "Leave or I will call the cops!" The man held his ground and showed no sign of being scared of the cops. Sarah then let out some more slack on the leash and Jesus would not let the man anywhere close to her. She followed this by saying "If you don't leave, I'm going to release my dog." This unlike the threat of police did scare the man and he tucked tail and ran away down the street, eventually disappearing into the darkness.

Who knows what would have happened to Sarah if her Pitbull wasn't there. The man who was evidently watching her through her window may have had more in mind than just watching and her Pitbull Jesus likely saved her from being raped or killed that night.

Stubby the War Dog

This story is from WWI and is probably one of the better known stories about Pitbulls.

During WWI a homeless Pitbull wandered into a training camp for the Armies 102nd Infantry. The soldiers immediately bonded with him and decided to keep him as their mascot. They named him Stubby because he had short legs. Later in October 1917 the 102nd Infantry was shipped out to France and they smuggled Stubby on to the S. S. Minnesota with them, inside an overcoat. He kept the soldiers company and was able sense danger much earlier than any of his owners. Stubby was known to wake guards up and let them know an attack was coming. He would work his way up and down the line and raise the morale of troops as well as keep constant watch. Later on during an attack, Stubby was injured by a German grenade and earned a Purple Heart. Stubby also found a German spy and pinned him by biting his pants until he was fully captured by US soldiers. One of the things Stubby is most known for is alerting the 102nd to a surprise mustard gas attack and possibly saving their lives. During the war Stubby was gassed several times and was temporarily hospitalized at one time. When the 102nd returned home they smuggled him home with them the same way they had smuggled him the first time.

When Stubby got home he was a celebrity and many newspapers covered his story. He was made a lifetime member of the American Legion and marched in every legion parade until he died. Stubby met and was honored by three US presidents. Later, General Blackjack Pershing gave Stubby the Gold Hero Dog's Medal.

In 1926 Stubby passed on and his Obituary in the New York Times was three columns wide and a half page long. This was much more than most famous people of the day were given. He now rests at the Smithsonian Institute in Washington D.C. and has his own exhibit there as well as one in the 102nd regimental museum in Connecticut.

There's much more to this story than what has been written here. Several books were written about Stubby and his life as the Hero War Dog.

Conclusion

While this book is a great guide for anyone who owns or wishes to own a Pitbull, there are some things you have to learn from experience. Once you get a Pitbull you will see why many people refuse to own any other breed of dog. They are great for cuddling and amazing at work and play.

Now that you've read this book you can safely say that you know more about Pitbulls than 99% of the people on earth. There is more information about them and for specific information on things such as competing you should go to the websites of some of the organizations that hold the competitions such as the IWPA or International Weight Pull Association.

Have fun with your Pitbull and never take him/her for granted....

Made in United States
Orlando, FL
17 April 2023

32185033R00036